Curious Compassion

A Journal to Sustainable Accountability

First published by Rainmaker Publishing 2024
Savannah, GA 31421
www.timetogetpublished.com

Paperback ISBN: 978-1-961351-28-8
First Edition
Journal Editing: Angela Pekalski & Heather Asiyanbi
Interior customized and prepared by Rainmaker Publishing

Introduction

Welcome to your journey toward sustainable accountability—an approach that honors your well-being while helping you show up for others with integrity and presence.

Accountability has become a popular buzzword, but all too often, it's tied to a rigid, corporate-style mindset that judges by emphasizing blame, guilt, and punishment.

This type of accountability can feel heavy, focusing on what went wrong rather than on how we can grow and thrive. But it can be so much more when you practice it with curiosity, compassion, and a focus on sustainable self-care.

The key difference is curiosity. When we approach self-awareness with a spirit of interest and exploration instead of judgment, we can begin to see ourselves as we really are.

True accountability isn't about harsh self-discipline or beating ourselves up when we fall short. Discipline definitely plays a role, but it's not the whole picture. In fact, when we rely solely on discipline, we risk pushing ourselves to exhaustion, stress, and even burnout.

When practiced with care, accountability is about learning to respect our needs and live in alignment with our values. It helps us navigate our goals and responsibilities in a way that allows us to get out of survival mode and thrive.

This workbook introduces a holistic, compassionate approach grounded in five foundational pillars:

1. **Self-Acceptance through Compassion and Gentle Self-Care**

    Everything begins here. Before we can hold ourselves accountable, we need to cultivate self-acceptance. This means embracing who we are, flaws and all. It's about recognizing that perfection isn't the goal— authenticity and self-compassion are.

    Learning to treat ourselves with kindness and care is the essential foundation upon which sustainable accountability is built. If we don't take care of ourselves, how can we truly be there for anyone else?

2. **Honest Self-Examination**

    Once we establish a foundation of self-compassion, we begin the work of honest self-examination. This is where accountability starts to take root.

    Honest self-reflection is about asking the tough questions: Why do I make the choices I make? What patterns keep showing up in my life? What values are guiding my actions?

    This step helps us dig deeper and see the truth of our behaviors and motivations. Without self-awareness, it's impossible to hold ourselves accountable in a meaningful way.

3. **Self-Awareness**

    Self-awareness grows out of honest self-examination. As we check in with ourselves, we develop a clearer understanding of who we are. We start to notice patterns in our behavior, our triggers, and the ways in which our choices align—or don't align—with our true values.

    Self-awareness allows us to pause, reflect, and make more intentional choices. It's the key to holding ourselves accountable in a way that feels authentic and empowering, rather than forced.

4. **Gentle, Loving, Realistic Self-Discipline**

   This is where self-discipline comes into play, but not in the traditional sense of rigid control. Gentle, loving, realistic self-discipline is about creating healthy boundaries and setting achievable goals that honor who we are and where we're at.

   When we approach discipline with compassion, it becomes a tool for growth, rather than a source of stress or self-punishment. It allows us to follow through on the commitments we make to ourselves—without the pressure of perfectionism or burnout.

5. **Sustainable Accountability**

   Finally, we arrive at sustainable accountability. When we practice self-acceptance, cultivate self-awareness, and approach discipline with care, we create a space where accountability supports us, rather than weighs us down. This kind of accountability is nourishing.

   It helps us grow while respecting our basic needs. It allows us to be present for others because we've first learned to show up for ourselves. Sustainable accountability isn't about ticking boxes or meeting every expectation—it's about living in alignment with your values, staying connected to your well-being, and being realistic about what you can give.

This workbook is designed to guide you through each of these five pillars, helping you redefine accountability on your own terms. You'll find daily reflection prompts, weekly check-ins, and deeper monthly and quarterly reviews. Each exercise is crafted to help you explore where you are now and make adjustments that reflect your true needs and goals.

Along the way, you'll discover that accountability isn't something that depletes you—it's something that supports and sustains you. You'll learn to show up for yourself and others in a way that feels balanced and aligned with who you are.

And, perhaps most importantly, you'll begin to see accountability as a compassionate practice—one that allows you to grow, adapt, and thrive, rather than a rigid standard you must meet.

How to Use This Workbook

1. **Daily Prompts:** These are designed to help you reflect on your day and your actions, cultivating compassionate self-awareness.

2. **Willing Exploration:** If you find resistance when answering questions, congratulations! You've just found blockage! Examine what makes you hesitate and write about that instead. The point is to learn about ourselves and question everything, including our own self image.

3. **Weekly Reflections:** At the end of each week, reflect on how accountability has shown up for you. This isn't about judging your progress but about gently noticing how you've met your own needs and where you can adjust going forward.

4. **Monthly Reflections:** At the close of each month, take a deeper look at your accountability practice. How have your habits supported your well-being? Where can you offer yourself more kindness, and what small changes might align you more with your own values?

5. **Revisiting Questions:** After the first 30 days, the questions will repeat for the next 60. Don't be concerned about repetition—your answers will

likely evolve as your self-awareness grows. Use this as an opportunity to dig deeper and explore new layers of understanding.

6. **Quarterly Reflections:** At the conclusion of the 90 days, you'll be invited to zoom out and ask the bigger questions: How do your actions align with your current values and your evolving definition of success? This is your chance to reassess your long-term goals with curiosity and openness.

7. **Flexibility in Practice:** There's no need to follow a rigid timeline. Life is unpredictable, and this workbook is here to support you on your own terms. If you miss a day, your journal doesn't have to hold the memory of this missed day forever; simply pick up where you left off. Progress isn't linear, and circular growth is part of the journey.

8. **Final Thoughts:** Don't feel as though you must begin this reflection journal on a Sunday or a Monday or even on the first day of the month. Your 30 days will be different from someone else's 30 days because your start date is the day of your choosing and isn't dictated by a calendar.

This journal is a living document, evolving as you do. By approaching accountability with curiosity, compassion, and self-awareness, you'll build a practice that sustains your personal and professional growth—without the burnout.

Core Values List

Your Guiding Values: Anchoring Your Accountability Journey

Directions for the list:

Your values are what guides your choices and actions, grounding your practice of sustainable accountability. Below is a list of words commonly associated with values. Before you begin your journey, identify your core values to remind you what truly matters to you as you reflect on the questions.

This exercise is not about imposing limits but exploring what drives your most authentic self, so you hold yourself accountable with compassion, awareness, and realism. Let your values be your guide as you build a life aligned with who you are and who you see yourself becoming.

○ Authenticity	○ Faith	○ Openness
○ Achievement	○ Fame	○ Optimism
○ Adventure	○ Friendships	○ Peace
○ Authority	○ Fun	○ Pleasure
○ Autonomy	○ Growth	○ Poise
○ Balance	○ Happiness	○ Popularity
○ Beauty	○ Honesty	○ Recognition
○ Boldness	○ Humor	○ Religion
○ Compassion	○ Influence	○ Reputation
○ Challenge	○ Inner Harmony	○ Respect
○ Citizenship	○ Justice	○ Responsibility
○ Community	○ Kindness	○ Security
○ Competency	○ Knowledge	○ Self-Respect
○ Contribution	○ Leadership	○ Service
○ Creativity	○ Learning	○ Spirituality
○ Curiosity	○ Love	○ Stability
○ Determination	○ Loyalty	○ Success
○ Fairness	○ Meaningful Work	○ Status

○ Trustworthiness   ○ ....   ○ ....
○ Wealth   ○ ....   ○ ....
○ Wisdom   ○ ....   ○ ....

Values & Decisions

- What does success in my personal life look like to me right now?

  ....
  ....

- How well am I living in alignment with these values, and what needs adjustment?

  ....
  ....

Setting New Goals

- What are three specific goals for the next 90 days that align with my redefined sense of accountability?

  ....
  ....

- What are the key actions I need to take to achieve these goals while maintaining balance?

  ....
  ....

A&A

DAY 1-30

Day 1

Acceptance & Compassion

How did I offer myself acceptance and compassion today?

_____

_____

_____

_____

_____

_____

When did I miss an opportunity to offer myself acceptance and compassion?

_____

_____

_____

_____

_____

_____

_____/_____/_____

Day 2

Honest Self-Examination

What choice did I make today that needs to be examined more closely?

What choice did I make that respected my needs?

......./......./........

Day 3

Self-Awareness

What did I notice about myself today that surprised me?

_____/_____/_____

Day 4

Realistic Self-Discipline

How can I balance self-discipline and self-kindness today?

_____

_____

_____

_____

_____

_____

_____

_____

_____

_____

_____

_____

_____

_____

_____

_____

____/____/_____

Day 5

Accountability in Action

How did I show accountability to myself and others today?

....
....
....
....
....
....
....

When did I miss an opportunity to show accountability to myself and others today?

....
....
....
....
....
....
....

......../......../...........

Day 6

Self-Care Reflection

Did I prioritize my needs today?

....

....

....

....

What helped me choose me?

....

....

....

....

When I didn't, what made me choose not to?

....

....

....

....

......../......../........

Day 7

Check-In

What was my biggest win this week in terms of responding instead of reacting?

Was there an opportunity to respond differently?

_____/_____/_____

Day 8

Acceptance & Compassion

How am I practicing self-acceptance in difficult moments? What can help me make it easier?

_____

_____

_____

_____

_____

_____

Did I miss an opportunity to practice self-acceptance today?

_____

_____

_____

_____

_____

_____

_____

_____/_____/_____

Day 9

Honest Self-Examination

When did I act out of habit today? How could I have responded differently?

....

....

....

....

....

....

When did I choose to respond differently today instead of falling into old patterns?

....

....

....

....

....

....

......../ ..../ ....

 Day 10

Self-Awareness

Am I being honest with myself about my current state of mind?

If not, what old habits and belief systems are preventing self-honesty?

____/____/_____

Day 11

Realistic Self-Discipline

Where did I push too hard today, and how can I adjust for tomorrow?

_____
_____
_____
_____
_____
_____

When did I give myself grace today and how did that feel?

_____
_____
_____
_____
_____
_____
_____

___/___/___

Day 12

Accountability in Action

What questions can I ask myself today to be more accountable tomorrow?

___/___/___

Day 13

Self-Care Reflection

How did I take care of myself today, emotionally or physically?

What opportunity did I miss to take care of myself today?

____/____/____

Day 14

Check-In

What's one lesson I can take into next week to make self-accountability easier?

....

....

....

....

....

....

....

What challenges did I face this week, and how did I respond to them?

....

....

....

....

....

....

....

....

____/____/_____

Day 15

Acceptance & Compassion

How was I gentle with myself today?

How was I too hard on myself today?

_____/_____/_____

Day 16

Honest Self-Examination

Did I take time to check in with my motives today? Why or why not?

_____/_____/_____

Day 17

Self-Awareness

What's one area where I lack self-awareness, and how can I work on it?

....

....

....

....

....

....

....

Feel free to ask close friends or family if an answer isn't readily available to you.

....

....

....

....

....

....

......../......./............

Day 18

Realistic Self-Discipline

Did I honor my energy levels today when making decisions?

_____

_____

_____

_____

_____

_____

_____

_____

_____

_____

_____

_____

_____

_____

_____

_____

____/____/____

Accountability in Action

What can I include in my morning ritual that will make accountability
easier throughout the day?

_____ / _____ / _____

Day 20

Self-Care Reflection

How did I set boundaries to protect my energy today? How did that work out/feel?

....

....

....

....

....

....

When did I miss an opportunity to set boundaries today? How did that work out/feel?

....

....

....

....

....

....

......../......../..............

Day 21

Check-In

What habit or mindset do I want to build on next week?

_____

_____

_____

_____

_____

_____

How did I practice compassion and self-care in moments of difficulty?

_____

_____

_____

_____

_____

_____

_____

_____/_____/_____

Day 22

Acceptance & Compassion

How did I show myself compassion when things didn't go as planned?

_____

_____

_____

_____

_____

_____

When did I miss an opportunity to show myself compassion?

_____

_____

_____

_____

_____

_____

_____

_____/_____/_____

Day 23

Honest Self-Examination

What choices today reflected my values?

_____
_____
_____
_____
_____
_____
_____

What choices didn't?

_____
_____
_____
_____
_____
_____
_____

_____/_____/_____

 Day 24

Self-Awareness

Did I listen to my emotions today? How did that affect my decisions?

_____/_____/_____

Realistic Self-Discipline

How did I balance structure and flexibility today?

_____/_____/_____

Day 26

Accountability in Action

Did I take time to explore all my options before making decisions today?

_____

_____

_____

_____

_____

_____

_____

_____

_____

_____

_____

_____

_____

_____

_____

_____

_____

____/____/_____

Day 27

Self-Care Reflection

What was my biggest act of self-care today?

How did I neglect my needs today?

_____/_____/_____

Day 28

Check-In

What's one thing I can adjust next week to make it easier to stay aligned with my goals?

....
....
....
....
....
....

In what ways did I show accountability for my own well-being and goals?

....
....
....
....
....
....
....

......../......../........

Day 29

Acceptance & Compassion

What did I struggle to accept today, and how can I practice more self-compassion?

_____

_____

_____

_____

_____

_____

_____

What did I find easier to accept than usual today?

_____

_____

_____

_____

_____

_____

_____

____/____/_____

 Day 30

Honest Self-Examination

What internal roadblocks got in my way today, and how can I work through them?

____/ ____/ _____

30-Day Check-In

1. How have I practiced self-compassion and acceptance this month, especially during moments of challenge or resistance?

----

2. What patterns am I noticing in how I show up for myself? Am I consistent, or am I asking/expecting too much of myself?

DAY 31-60

Day 1

Acceptance & Compassion

How did I offer myself acceptance and compassion today?

....

....

....

....

....

....

....

When did I miss an opportunity to offer myself acceptance and compassion?

....

....

....

....

....

....

....

......../......../...............

Day 2

Honest Self-Examination

What choice did I make today that needs to be examined more closely?

....

....

....

....

....

....

What choice did I make that respected my needs?

....

....

....

....

....

....

....

......../......../........

Day 3

Self-Awareness

What did I notice about myself today that surprised me?

_____

_____

_____

_____

_____

_____

_____

_____

_____

_____

_____

_____

_____

_____

_____

_____

_____

____/____/_____

Day 4

Realistic Self-Discipline

How can I balance self-discipline and self-kindness today?

_____

_____

_____

_____

_____

_____

_____

_____

_____

_____

_____

_____

_____

_____

_____

_____

_____

____/ ____/ _____

Day 5

Accountability in Action

How did I show accountability to myself and others today?

_____

_____

_____

_____

_____

_____

_____

When did I miss an opportunity to show accountability to myself and others today?

_____

_____

_____

_____

_____

_____

____/____/_____

Day 6

Self-Care Reflection

Did I prioritize my needs today?

....

....

....

....

What helped me choose me?

....

....

....

....

When I didn't, what made me choose not to?

....

....

....

....

......../......../............

Day 7

Check-In

What was my biggest win this week in terms of responding instead of reacting?

....

....

....

....

....

....

Was there an opportunity to respond differently?

....

....

....

....

....

....

....

......../......../............

Day 8

Acceptance & Compassion

How am I practicing self-acceptance in difficult moments? What can help me make it easier?

_____

_____

_____

_____

_____

_____

_____

Did I miss an opportunity to practice self-acceptance today?

_____

_____

_____

_____

_____

_____

_____

____/____/_____

Day 9

Honest Self-Examination

When did I act out of habit today? How could I have responded differently?

When did I choose to respond differently today instead of falling into old patterns?

_____/_____/_____

 Day 10

Self-Awareness

Am I being honest with myself about my current state of mind?

....

....

....

....

....

....

If not, what old habits and belief systems are preventing self-honesty?

....

....

....

....

....

....

....

......./......./.........

Realistic Self-Discipline

Where did I push too hard today, and how can I adjust for tomorrow?

_____

_____

_____

_____

_____

_____

_____

_____

When did I give myself grace today and how did that feel?

_____

_____

_____

_____

_____

_____

_____

_____

_____ / _____ / _____

 Day 12

Accountability in Action

What questions can I ask myself today to be more accountable tomorrow?

_____/_____/_____

Day 13

Self-Care Reflection

How did I take care of myself today, emotionally or physically?

_____

_____

_____

_____

_____

_____

_____

What opportunity did I miss to take care of myself today?

_____

_____

_____

_____

_____

_____

_____

_____/_____/_____

Day 14

Check-In

What's one lesson I can take into next week to make self-accountability easier?

_____

_____

_____

_____

_____

_____

What challenges did I face this week, and how did I respond to them?

_____

_____

_____

_____

_____

_____

_____

_____

......../ ..../ ....

Day 15

Acceptance & Compassion

How was I gentle with myself today?

_____

_____

_____

_____

_____

_____

How was I too hard on myself today?

_____

_____

_____

_____

_____

_____

_____

_____/_____/_____

Day 16

Honest Self-Examination

Did I take time to check in with my motives today? Why or why not?

_____

_____

_____

_____

_____

_____

_____

_____

_____

_____

_____

_____

_____

_____

_____

_____

_____

_____

____/____/_____

Self-Awareness

What's one area where I lack self-awareness, and how can I work on it?

Feel free to ask close friends or family if an answer isn't readily available to you.

____/____/_____

 Day 18

Realistic Self-Discipline

Did I honor my energy levels today when making decisions?

_____/_____/_____

Day 19

Accountability in Action

What can I include in my morning ritual that will make accountability easier throughout the day?

_____

_____

_____

_____

_____

_____

_____

_____

_____

_____

_____

_____

_____

_____

_____

_____

_____

____/____/____

 Day 20

Self-Care Reflection

How did I set boundaries to protect my energy today? How did that work out/feel?

....

....

....

....

....

....

When did I miss an opportunity to set boundaries today? How did that work out/feel?

....

....

....

....

....

....

......../......../............

Day 21

Check-In

What habit or mindset do I want to build on next week?

_____

_____

_____

_____

_____

_____

_____

How did I practice compassion and self-care in moments of difficulty?

_____

_____

_____

_____

_____

_____

___/___/___

Day 22

Acceptance & Compassion

How did I show myself compassion when things didn't go as planned?

_____
_____
_____
_____
_____
_____
_____

When did I miss an opportunity to show myself compassion?

_____
_____
_____
_____
_____
_____
_____
_____

____/____/____

Day 23

Honest Self-Examination

What choices today reflected my values?

What choices didn't?

___/___/___

Day 24

Self-Awareness

Did I listen to my emotions today? How did that affect my decisions?

_____/_____/_____

Day 25

Realistic Self-Discipline

How did I balance structure and flexibility today?

_____

_____

_____

_____

_____

_____

_____

_____

_____

_____

_____

_____

_____

_____

_____

_____

_____

_____

......./......./...............

 Day 26

Accountability in Action

Did I take time to explore all my options before making decisions today?

....

....

....

....

....

....

....

....

....

....

....

....

....

....

....

....

......../......../........

Day 27

Self-Care Reflection

What was my biggest act of self-care today?

How did I neglect my needs today?

____/____/_____

 Day 28

Check-In

What's one thing I can adjust next week to make it easier to stay aligned with my goals?

....
....
....
....
....
....

In what ways did I show accountability for my own well-being and goals?

....
....
....
....
....
....
....
....

......../......./..........

Acceptance & Compassion

What did I struggle to accept today, and how can I practice more self-compassion?

What did I find easier to accept than usual today?

____/____/____

Day 30

Honest Self-Examination

What internal roadblocks got in my way today, and how can I work through them?

....

....

....

....

....

....

....

....

....

....

....

....

....

....

....

....

........../........./.............

60-Day Check-In

1. Where have I felt resistance to accountability, and what can I learn about myself by exploring that resistance?

2. Am I taking enough time for self-assessment? Am I questioning and adjusting my goals when necessary, or am I stuck in old patterns that no longer serve me?

DAY 61-90

Day 1

Acceptance & Compassion

How did I offer myself acceptance and compassion today?

_____

_____

_____

_____

_____

_____

_____

When did I miss an opportunity to offer myself acceptance and compassion?

_____

_____

_____

_____

_____

_____

_____/_____/_____

Day 2

Honest Self-Examination

What choice did I make today that needs to be examined more closely?

....

....

....

....

....

....

What choice did I make that respected my needs?

....

....

....

....

....

....

....

........../........../..........

Day 3

Self-Awareness

What did I notice about myself today that surprised me?

_____ / _____ / _____

Day 4

Realistic Self-Discipline

How can I balance self-discipline and self-kindness today?

_____

_____

_____

_____

_____

_____

_____

_____

_____

_____

_____

_____

_____

_____

_____

_____

_____

_____

____/____/_____

Day 5

Accountability in Action

How did I show accountability to myself and others today?

....

....

....

....

....

....

When did I miss an opportunity to show accountability to myself and others today?

....

....

....

....

....

....

....

___/___/___

Day 6

Self-Care Reflection

Did I prioritize my needs today?

....

....

....

....

What helped me choose me?

....

....

....

....

When I didn't, what made me choose not to?

....

....

....

....

_____/_____/_____

Day 7

Check-In

What was my biggest win this week in terms of responding instead of reacting?

_____

_____

_____

_____

_____

_____

Was there an opportunity to respond differently?

_____

_____

_____

_____

_____

_____

_____

_____

_____/_____/_____

Day 8

Acceptance & Compassion

How am I practicing self-acceptance in difficult moments? What can help me make it easier?

_____

_____

_____

_____

_____

_____

Did I miss an opportunity to practice self-acceptance today?

_____

_____

_____

_____

_____

_____

_____

_____

____/____/_____

Day 9

Honest Self-Examination

When did I act out of habit today? How could I have responded differently?

_____

_____

_____

_____

_____

_____

When did I choose to respond differently today instead of falling into old patterns?

_____

_____

_____

_____

_____

_____

____/____/____

 Day 10

Self-Awareness

Am I being honest with myself about my current state of mind?

_____

_____

_____

_____

_____

_____

_____

If not, what old habits and belief systems are preventing self-honesty?

_____

_____

_____

_____

_____

_____

_____

_____/_____/_____

Day 11

Realistic Self-Discipline

Where did I push too hard today, and how can I adjust for tomorrow?

....

....

....

....

....

....

When did I give myself grace today and how did that feel?

....

....

....

....

....

....

......../......../............

Day 12

Accountability in Action

What questions can I ask myself today to be more accountable tomorrow?

....

....

....

....

....

....

....

....

....

....

....

....

....

....

....

....

....

....

....

........../........../..........

Day 13

Self-Care Reflection

How did I take care of myself today, emotionally or physically?

_____

_____

_____

_____

_____

_____

_____

What opportunity did I miss to take care of myself today?

_____

_____

_____

_____

_____

_____

_____

____/____/____

Day 14

Check-In

What's one lesson I can take into next week to make self-accountability easier?

_____

_____

_____

_____

_____

_____

What challenges did I face this week, and how did I respond to them?

_____

_____

_____

_____

_____

_____

_____

_____

_____/_____/_____

Day 15

Acceptance & Compassion

How was I gentle with myself today?

How was I too hard on myself today?

_____/_____/_____

Day 16

Honest Self-Examination

Did I take time to check in with my motives today? Why or why not?

_____

_____

_____

_____

_____

_____

_____

_____

_____

_____

_____

_____

_____

_____

_____

_____

_____

_____

_____

_____

_____

_____/_____/_____

Self-Awareness

What's one area where I lack self-awareness, and how can I work on it?

Feel free to ask close friends or family if an answer isn't readily available to you.

......./......./............

Day 18

Realistic Self-Discipline

Did I honor my energy levels today when making decisions?

_____/_____/_____

Day 19

Accountability in Action

What can I include in my morning ritual that will make accountability easier throughout the day?

_____

_____

_____

_____

_____

_____

_____

_____

_____

_____

_____

_____

_____

_____

_____

_____

_____

___/___/___

Day 20

Self-Care Reflection

How did I set boundaries to protect my energy today? How did that work out/feel?

When did I miss an opportunity to set boundaries today? How did that work out/feel?

......../........./...........

Day 21

Check-In

What habit or mindset do I want to build on next week?

How did I practice compassion and self-care in moments of difficulty?

_____/_____/_____

Day 22

Acceptance & Compassion

How did I show myself compassion when things didn't go as planned?

_____

_____

_____

_____

_____

_____

When did I miss an opportunity to show myself compassion?

_____

_____

_____

_____

_____

_____

_____

___/___/___

Day 23

Honest Self-Examination

What choices today reflected my values?

What choices didn't?

_____/_____/_____

Day 24

Self-Awareness

Did I listen to my emotions today? How did that affect my decisions?

_____/_____/_____

Realistic Self-Discipline

How did I balance structure and flexibility today?

_____

_____

_____

_____

_____

_____

_____

_____

_____

_____

_____

_____

_____

_____

_____

_____

_____

____/____/____

Day 26

Accountability in Action

Did I take time to explore all my options before making decisions today?

_____

_____

_____

_____

_____

_____

_____

_____

_____

_____

_____

_____

_____

_____

_____

_____

_____

_____

____/____/_____

Day 27

Self-Care Reflection

What was my biggest act of self-care today?

How did I neglect my needs today?

_____/_____/_____

Day 28

Check-In

What's one thing I can adjust next week to make it easier to stay aligned with my goals?

....

....

....

....

....

....

In what ways did I show accountability for my own well-being and goals?

....

....

....

....

....

....

....

......./......./.............

Day 29

Acceptance & Compassion

What did I struggle to accept today, and how can I practice more self-compassion?

_____

_____

_____

_____

_____

What did I find easier to accept than usual today?

_____

_____

_____

_____

_____

_____/_____/_____

 Day 30

Honest Self-Examination

What internal roadblocks got in my way today, and how can I work through them?

_____/_____/_____

90-Day Check-In

1. In what ways have I honored my personal boundaries this month, and how has that contributed to my well-being?

2. What areas of my life need more compassion and gentler discipline? What's one new habit or mindset I'd like to focus on for the next 30 days to support this growth?

CLOSING
REFLECTIONS

Reassessing Success

- What does success in my *personal* life look like to me right now? How has that changed over the course of this journey?

- What does success in my *professional* life look like to me? How aligned is my work with my personal values?

This is Farewell, not Goodbye

This journal may be complete, but your journey continues.

This is not a final step but more of a pause on a much longer, almost never-ending journey of self-awareness, compassion, and accountability. The lessons you've explored—self-acceptance, gentle self-care, and honest self-examination—are tools you'll carry with you as you continue reflecting and growing in your sustainable accountability habit.

Through the practice of compassionate self-assessment, you've deepened your self-awareness, understanding more about who you are and what you need to thrive. You are empowered to approach self-discipline in a way that is realistic, loving, and sustainable.

It's no longer about perfection or productivity—it's about honoring your well-being, allowing you to show up fully for yourself and, by extension, for others. True accountability begins with you respecting your own boundaries and needs to create space to offer the same respect and care to others.

This isn't about being productive every moment of every day—none of us are machines. It's about living in alignment with your values, cultivating habits that support your growth, and, most importantly, treating yourself with kindness along the way.

As you move forward, know that this is not the end of your reflection, but an ongoing practice. You've built a foundation of self-compassion and self-awareness—trust it, revisit it, and allow it to guide you as you navigate the changes and challenges ahead.

There will be moments of resistance, and that's okay. Greet them with curiosity and openness, knowing they hold valuable insights.

Finally, be gentle with yourself, embrace the ebb and flow, and trust that accountability isn't a destination—it's a relationship with yourself, and you will nurture it for the rest of your life.

About Anik

As an autistic, non-binary individual, Anik never quite fit the traditional business mold. Their combination of keen observation skills (thanks, trauma) and lessons learned (thanks, burnout) helped them provide much-needed guidance for their bookkeeping clients. So they founded A&A Business Associates to help overwhelmed business owners finally create a balanced business, by blending Sustainable Accountability Coaching with CFO and accounting services. Learn more at aabusinessassociates. com.

Made in the USA
Columbia, SC
16 June 2025

59286903R00069